JUL - - 2007

D1278739

HORSEPOWER

HOVERCRAFTS

by Aaron Sautter

Reading Consultant:

Barbara J. Fox

Reading Specialist

North Carolina State University

Content Consultant:

Marquis Songer

President, Hoverclub of America Inc.

Capstone
press®

Mankato, Minnesota

Blazers is published by Capstone Press,
151 Good Counsel Drive, P.O. Box 669, Mankato, Minnesota 56002.
www.capstonepress.com

Library of Congress Cataloging-in-Publication Data
Sautter, Aaron.
    Hovercrafts / by Aaron Sautter.
    p. cm.—(Blazers. Horsepower)
    Summary: "Describes hovercrafts, their main features, and how they are
raced"—Provided by publisher.
    Includes bibliographical references and index.
    ISBN-13: 978-0-7368-6782-5 (hardcover)
    ISBN-10: 0-7368-6782-1 (hardcover)
    1. Ground-effect machines—Juvenile literature. 2. Motorboat racing—
Juvenile literature. I. Title. II. Series.
VM363.S38 2007
629.3—dc22   2006020953

Editorial Credits
Jenny Marks, editor; Jason Knudson, set designer; Patrick Dentinger,
    book designer; Jo Miller, photo researcher/photo editor

Photo Credits
Art Directors/John M Pim, 28–29
Corbis/Carl & Ann Purcell, 11; Geoffrey Taunton; Cordaiy Photo Library Ltd., 23
Gary R. Jensen, 5, 8, 20
Getty Images Inc./AFP/Johannes Eisele, 24, 25; Allsport/Stu Forster, 13
Index Stock Imagery/Volvox, 19
NeotericHovercraft.com, 14
Photo by: Pro Photo Productions, cover, 6, 7, 15, 16–17, 21
SuperStock/Buzz Pictures, 12
U.S. Marine Corps photo by Lance Cpl. Scott L. Eberle, 26
U.S. Navy Photo by PHAN Joshua T. Rodriguez, 27

1 2 3 4 5 6 12 11 10 09 08 07

TABLE OF CONTENTS

RACING ON AIR

Drivers rev growling engines at the starting line. The flag drops, and hovercrafts roar off toward the river.

The hovercrafts rumble across
the water. One driver suddenly loses
control. His craft spins off course.
Craft 45 swerves to avoid a crash.

Without a scratch, number 45 speeds back to shore. The daring driver gives the engine full power.

Number 45 races far ahead of
the pack. The finish line is in sight.
In a blaze of speed, the driver
wins the race.

DESIGN

Hovercrafts cruise on a cushion of air. A powerful fan pushes air below the craft. The skirt traps the air in place so the craft floats over any surface.

Skirt

Thrust propeller

The thrust propeller blasts air
to push the craft forward. Rudders
attached to the propeller control
which direction the craft moves.

BLAZER FACT

Skilled drivers can steer small hovercrafts by shifting their body weight.

Hovercrafts do not have brakes. To stop, drivers give less power to the engine or turn the handlebars 180 degrees at full power.

BLAZER FACT

A handlebar is connected to the rudders. Drivers use the handlebar to steer the craft.

HOVERCRAFT PARTS

Thrust duct

Thrust propeller

Rudders

Hull

Windshield

Lift fan

IL 4708 JV

Skirt

SPEED AND SAFETY

Powerful hovercrafts quickly pick up speed. Some crafts can go from 0 to 60 miles per hour (0 to 97 kilometers per hour) in about 5 seconds.

Racing drivers face real dangers on hovercrafts. Goggles and helmets protect drivers in a crash. Drivers wear life jackets in case their crafts flip in the water.

Some hovercrafts reach speeds of 65 miles per hour (105 kilometers per hour) or more.

HOVERCRAFTS IN ACTION

Deep oceans, thin ice, and sandy deserts are no match for hovercrafts. Only steep hills and cliffs can stop these vehicles.

Hovercraft races test the skills of drivers all around the world. Thrilled fans watch drivers tackle courses that curve across land and water.

Hovercrafts aren't only used for fun. Military crafts quickly aid victims of disasters. From rescues to races, hovercrafts take on any task!

BLAZER FACT

Hovercrafts rescued victims and delivered supplies to Indonesia after the 2004 tsunami.

UNSTOPPABLE!

GLOSSARY

cushion (KUSH-uhn)—a thick layer used to support something; hovercrafts ride on a cushion of air to avoid touching the ground.

life jacket (LIFE JAK-it)—a device to keep you afloat if you fall in the water

rev (REV)—to make an engine run quickly and noisily

rudder (RUHD-ur)—a hinged plate attached to the back of a hovercraft that is used for steering

skirt (SKURT)—a piece of rubber or coated nylon attached to the bottom of a hovercraft to help create a cushion of air

steer (STEER)—to make a vehicle go in a particular direction

tsunami (tsoo-NAH-mee)—a very large wave

READ MORE

Holzer, David. *Hover Power.* Learn About. Suffolk, UK: Top That! Kids, 2005.

Hopping, Lorraine Jean. *Hovercrafts.* Flight Test Lab. San Diego: Silver Dolphin Books, 2004.

Will, Sandra. *Transportation Inventions: From Subways to Submarines.* Which Came First? New York: Bearport, 2006.

INTERNET SITES

FactHound offers a safe, fun way to find Internet sites related to this book. All of the sites on FactHound have been researched by our staff.

Here's how:
1. Visit *www.facthound.com*
2. Choose your grade level.
3. Type in this book ID **0736867821** for age-appropriate sites. You may also browse subjects by clicking on letters, or by clicking on pictures and words.
4. Click on the **Fetch It** button.

FactHound will fetch the best sites for you!

INDEX